Boys and Girls Playing

(and Other Addresses to Children)

by the Right Rev.
John Charles Ryle, D. D.
Lord Bishop of Liverpool
Author of *Expository Thoughts on the Gospels*

Soli Deo Gloria
...for instruction in righteousness...

Soli Deo Gloria Publications
P.O. Box 451, Morgan, PA 15064
(412) 221–1901/FAX 221–1902

*

Boys and Girls Playing and Other Addresses to Children
was published in New York by Robert Carter and
Brothers in 1881. This Soli Deo Gloria reprint,
in which spelling, grammar, and formatting
changes have been made, is © 1996 by
Don Kistler and Soli Deo Gloria.

*

ISBN 1–57358–046–5

Contents

Boys and Girls Playing

"The streets of the city shall be full of boys and girls playing." Zechariah 8:5

Dear children, the text at the top of this page is about things to come. God tells us what there will be one day in the streets of Jerusalem.

Jerusalem, you know, is a very famous place. It was the chief town of the Jews. It was the city where David and Solomon lived. It was the city where Christ died on the cross and rose again. All boys and girls who read the Bible know something about Jerusalem.

Jerusalem was once a very grand and rich town. In all the earth there was no city like it when the Jews feared God. But the sins of the Jews brought ruin on Jerusalem. It is now a poor, decayed, dirty place, and a sorrow to all who see it.

1

But a day shall yet come when Jerusalem shall be once more a grand and beautiful place. The Jews will one day repent and serve Christ and return to their own land. Then the good times of Jerusalem shall come back again. It shall be once more a great, rich, and prosperous city. And then the words of the text will come to pass: "The streets of the city shall be full of boys and girls playing."

Dear children, there are two things I want you to learn out of this text. You see God tells us that in the holiest, best days of Jerusalem there will be boys and girls playing in the streets. He tells us this, and He does not say that it is wrong. Let us see what we can make of this.

1. Learn for one thing that God thinks about boys and girls and notices what they do. He does not only tell us about the men and women of Jerusalem. He makes mention of the "boys and girls." He tells us it will be a good time when there are many of them, and that it will be a good time when

they play in the streets.

Some folks do not care to see children, and say that there are too many of them in the world. These folks are not like God. The great God in heaven loves children. He knows that there will be no men and women by and by if there are no children now. He says in Psalm 127:5, "Happy is the man who has his quiver full of children." Folks who do not like boys and girls, and are cross with them, ought to remember that they were once children themselves.

There is much about children in the Bible. Read the histories of Ishmael, Isaac, Benjamin, Moses, Samuel, and Abijah. Read the Proverbs of Solomon and see how often that wise man spoke of children. Read the Gospels and see how Jesus Christ noticed little infants and took them in His arms and blessed them. Read the epistles of the Apostle Paul and see how he speaks of children. These things were written for our learning.

Dear children, remember all this and do

not forget it. You are never too young or too little for God to take notice of you. You are never too young or too little to begin thinking of God. Are you old enough to be naughty? Then be sure that you are old enough to be good. Are you old enough to talk? Then be sure that you are old enough to say your prayers. Are you old enough to learn bad words? Then be sure that you are old enough to learn texts. Are you old enough to know and love your mother? Then be sure that you are old enough to know and love Jesus who died to save your souls.

Boys and girls, remember this first great lesson: God takes notice of you. Mind that you take notice of God.

2. Learn another thing from our text: God allows boys and girls to play. He does not tell us that the streets of Jerusalem shall be full of boys and girls sitting still and silent and idle. He tells us that the boys and girls shall be playing, and He teaches us that playing is not wrong.

Some good people seem to think that children should never play at all. They tell us that all games are sinful, and that boys and girls should always look very grave and never laugh or be merry. They make a great mistake when they say this. God tells us that in the good times of Jerusalem "boys and girls shall play in the streets." Then play in moderation cannot be wrong.

Play suits the age of boys and girls. They cannot be always learning lessons or working. Their minds are not strong enough for this. They are not like old people. They must have some time every day for rest and exercise.

Play helps children to grow healthy and strong. Their bodies will never be well if they are sitting still or standing from morning to night. They need all their limbs to be exercised while young if they are to be healthy men and women when they are old. It is natural to a child to play. The boy or girl who does not like play is generally not well.

Play teaches children to bear and for-bear, and to put up with disappointments. They cannot always win the game and have their own way. Play makes them ac-tive and keen-witted and ready for any-thing. They cannot succeed in games of skill unless they keep awake. The great Duke of Wellington used to say that he learned to win the battle of Waterloo when he was in the playing fields of Eton College.

Play makes boys and girls learn better when it is over. They come back to lessons sharper, quicker, and more clever than if they sat reading and writing all day long. Brains and nerves and mind are all better for play.

Play of any kind is better than idleness. "Satan always finds some work for idle hands to do." If boys and girls do not have some nice games to take to after school, they are quite sure to get into mischief.

Dear children, you see that I am a friend to your playing. I am not ashamed of being so, because I see that God approves of it.

God allows us to do anything except sin; and play in moderation is not sinful.

I shall now finish my sermon with four bits of advice to boys and girls, which I hope they will think about and not forget:

1. In all your play remember the eye and ear of God. He sees and hears everything. Dear children, say nothing you would not like God to hear; do nothing you would not like God to see.

2. In all your play, keep your temper. Be kind, cheerful, unselfish, and good-natured, even when you lose the game. Dear children, never fly into a passion. Whatever you play at, keep your temper.

3. Do not neglect work because of play. Let all your play help you to learn better, and to be a better boy or girl, both at school and home. It is quite true that "all work and no play makes a dull boy." But I believe it is no less true that all play and no work makes a stupid, useless man.

4. In the last place, never forget, even in

your play, that all true happiness comes from Christ. If you want to be happy boys and girls, love Christ and make Him your chief Friend. Christ is the giver of light hearts and peaceful minds. The happiest child is the child who loves Christ most.

There is a green hill far away,
Without a city wall,
Where the dear Lord was crucified,
Who died to save us all.

We do not know, we cannot tell,
What pains He had to bear,
But we believe it was for us
He hung and suffered there.

He died that we might be forgiven,
He died to make us good,
That we might go at last to heaven,
Saved by His precious blood.

There was no other good enough
To pay the price of sin;

He only could unlock the gate
Of heaven, and let us in.

Oh, dearly, dearly has He loved!
And we must love Him too,
And trust in His redeeming blood,
And try His works to do.

Seeking the Lord Early

"I love them that love Me; and those that seek Me early shall find Me." Proverbs 8:17

Dear children, I am going to talk to you about Jesus Christ and your souls.

I want to make you happy. But I know that people are never really happy unless their *souls* are happy; and I am sure that people's souls cannot be happy unless they love Jesus Christ. And that is the reason why I am going to preach to you now—I want to tell you something about Jesus Christ and your souls.

Dear children, I hope that you will all attend while I talk to you. I pray that the Spirit of God may come into your hearts and make you able to do so. Try to listen to me; try to understand what I say; try to remember and carry away something in your minds. I wish to do you all a great deal of good. Do not forget I am preaching to you—not to the grown-up people, but to you, only to you.

Now just think what a pleasant text we have here. It is said: "I love them that love Me; and those that seek Me early shall find Me."

These are sweet words indeed; and who do you think says them? They are said by the Lord Jesus Christ, the Son of God, the Savior of the world. He is called "Wisdom" in this chapter. But we know it means Jesus Christ, for there are things said about Wisdom in this chapter which cannot be said truly about anyone but Jesus Christ Himself. Come now and let us see what Jesus Christ says.

Listen, dear children, for this is very important.

1. He tells us: "I love them that love Me." Now what can we make out of this?

First of all, do you not think it is very pleasant to hear that there are people whom Jesus Christ loves? You know we all like to be loved in this world. Think how disagreeable it would be for you and me if there was nobody alive who loved us. Suppose that no man or woman cared a bit for us; suppose that everybody neglected us and left us alone. What would we do? We would be wretched, miserable, and unhappy! I am sure we all like to be loved.

Well, then, just consider what a blessed thing it must be to be loved by Jesus Christ, by the Son of God Himself.

You know that sometimes people love us in this world and yet can do nothing for us. Your dear fathers and mothers love you, but perhaps they are poor and cannot buy what you want; or perhaps they are sick and very old and can do nothing to help you.

But, dear children, these are things that can never happen to Jesus Christ, and I will tell you why:

Jesus Christ is very great. He is King of kings and Lord of lords. He is Maker of all things. He is God Himself. He is Almighty.

He is able to do anything He likes.

Oh, what a thing it must be to be loved by Jesus Christ!

And, again, Jesus Christ is very rich. He has everything to give away which you can want, either for soul or body. He keeps the keys of heaven. He has an endless store of blessings in His treasure house, far more than I could describe.

Oh, what a thing it must be to be loved by Jesus Christ!

And, again, Jesus Christ is very good. He never refuses anyone who asks Him favors in a proper way. He was never known to say "No!" to any person who made a prayer to Him with a meek and humble heart.

Oh, what a thing it must be to be loved by Jesus Christ!

Dear children, consider these things. Do you want a great friend? Do you want a rich friend? Do you want a kind friend? Is this the sort of friend you would like? Then be sure there is no friend in all the world like Jesus Christ. There is no love so much worth having as the love of Jesus Christ.

Blessed and happy are those whom Jesus Christ loves. I could not tell you a tenth part of all the great things He does for their souls.

He pardons all their sins. He forgives all the bad things they do. He washes them in His own blood and makes them whiter than snow, so that not a spot remains. Dear children, I think that is just what you and I want. We have all sinned many, many sins.

Besides, He gives them power to become good. He puts His Spirit in their hearts; and He makes them love God's ways and like to walk in them. Dear children, that, too, is just the thing you and I want. We have very bad, wicked hearts by nature. We never love God's ways of ourselves.

Besides this, He takes care that none whom He loves shall be lost. He keeps them as a shepherd keeps his sheep. He will not allow either wicked men or the devil to destroy their souls. Dear children, that, too, is just what you and I want. We are all very weak and foolish creatures. We would never be safe if left to ourselves.

And, last, He is getting ready a place in heaven for those whom He loves. He has a glorious house for them there, far away from sin, sorrow, and trouble. Dear children, that, too, is good news for you and me. Is it not pleasant to think He has prepared a home for us so that whenever we leave this world we shall go to a place of peace and rest?

All these things the Lord Jesus Christ does for those whom He loves. Look at them! What mighty things, what glorious things they are! He cleanses them from all their sins. He gives them power to be good. He takes care that they are not lost. He gets ready a house for them in heaven.

Dear children, this is love indeed; this is love worth having. Did I not tell you, truly there is nothing in all the world to be compared to Christ's love? There is nothing like being loved by Jesus Christ!

2. But let us see next who are those that Jesus Christ loves. He tells us in our text when He says, "I love those that love Me."

Now how shall we know whether we love Jesus Christ or not? This is indeed an important question. Are there no marks or signs, perhaps you will say, by which those who love Him may be found out? Yes, dear children, I think there are. And what those marks and signs are I shall now try to show you. Remember, then, for one thing, those who love Jesus Christ believe whatever He says in the Bible.

The Bible says we are all sinners—lost, perishing sinners, full of wickedness and deceit, deserving nothing but God's anger. Many people cannot quite believe this. They cannot bring themselves to think they are so bad—they dislike to be told of it. It is not so with those who love Jesus Christ. They believe it all; they are ready to say, "It is true, true, quite true."

Again, the Bible tells us we must come to Christ and trust only in Him if we would be saved. It says that nothing but His blood can wash away our sins, that it is only for His sake that anyone can be forgiven. Many people will not believe this either. They cannot imagine that their own goodness will not help to get them to heaven. But those who love Jesus Christ believe it all. They take the Lord at His word; they stop trusting in their own goodness and are ready to say, "None but Christ, none but Christ is my hope."

Dear children, no one can love Jesus Christ who does not believe what He says. Think what a sad thing it would be if you and I could not get our relations to believe us. Only fancy how hard and unkind it would seem if they were to say, "We do not depend at all on what you tell us; we cannot trust your word." I am sure we would suppose they no longer loved us. This, then, is one mark of those who love Jesus Christ: they never doubt what He tells them; they believe every word.

Remember, for another thing, those who love Jesus Christ try to please Him. You know when you love people in this world you try to please them. You try to do what they bid you, and to behave as they wish you, and to remember what they teach you, and to mind what they tell you. And why do you do so? Because you love them.

And besides this, you try and please them not only before their faces, when they can see you, but also when they are gone away and out of sight. True love makes you always think: "What would my dear friends like me to do?" If your father and mother found you doing naughty things, doing what they told you not to do, might they not well say, "Child, child, I am afraid you do not really love me"? Yes, indeed, they might. True love will always cause true obedience. And the Bible says: "Even a child is known by his doings" (Proverbs 20:11).

Now, dear children, just as you try to

please your friends if you love them, so those who love Jesus Christ try to please Him. They are always trying to do His will, to keep His laws, to live after His commandments, to obey His precepts. They do not think any of Christ's commands are grievous; they never say that His laws are hard, strict, and disagreeable. It is their *delight* to walk in His paths.

Dear children, no man, woman, or child can really love Jesus Christ if they do not try to obey Him. "You are My friends," He says in John 15:14, "if you do whatsoever I command you."

This, then, is another sure mark of those who love Jesus Christ: they try in all things to please Him.

Now we have gotten through one part of our text. Sit still and think for a moment about what you have heard. Each of you ask your own heart this little question: "Do I love Jesus Christ or not? Do I believe what He says, and do I try to please Him?" Those who can answer "Yes" are the children He especially loves. Oh, remember what He says: "I love those that love Me."

3. But let us look next to the other part of our text and see what we may learn from it. I really think this part is almost as pleasant as the first, for it contains a sweet promise: "Those that seek Me early shall find Me."

Dear children, how are you and I to seek Jesus Christ? He does not live upon earth like one of us; we cannot see Him with our eyes. We cannot reach Him and take hold of Him with our hands, and yet He says, "Those that seek Me shall find Me." What can this mean? Let me try to tell you.

First of all, you must seek Jesus Christ in His own book. The Bible is Jesus Christ's book, and all who want to know Him must be very diligent in reading their Bibles. He says to every one of you, "Search the Scriptures," and He will give the Holy Spirit to those who seek Him in the Scriptures and teach them all about Himself.

Dear children, be regular readers of the

Bible all your lives. Let the Word dwell in you richly and then you will be truly wise. Read it daily, read a great deal of it; try and remember it; learn texts by heart. I remember a little girl in my first parish who could learn seventy verses of the Bible in a week. How pleasant it is to find the Apostle Paul reminding Timothy that from a child he had known the Holy Scriptures! Now, why should not all of you be like Timothy in this? I would like to hear that you were all Bible-reading children, children who read the Bible at home as well as at school.

This, then, is one way to seek Jesus Christ. You must seek Him in the Bible.

Second, you must seek Jesus Christ in His own house. Jesus Christ has many houses in this country where people meet together to pray to Him and to hear about Him. This church is one of them, and wherever two or three are gathered together in Jesus Christ's name the Lord Himself is really present, though we cannot see Him with our eyes.

Dear children, I hope you will all regularly go to Jesus Christ's house as long as you live. I hope you will never do like those foolish people who keep away from it. Oh, what sad harm they are doing to their poor souls! And, when you go, try to attend to all you hear and to get good from it. Do not stare about and make noise or talk to other children, but listen well to all that is read or preached. Jesus Christ is there and He sees how you behave. He loves to see little children coming to His house and behaving well. If you persevere in so doing, you may be sure He will put His Spirit in you and fill you with all knowledge.

This, then, is another way to seek Jesus Christ. You must seek Him in His house.

Third, you must seek Jesus Christ on your knees in prayer. You must ask Him with your own mouth to give you everything that your soul wants. You must ask Him to cleanse you from all your sins in His blood, to give you His Spirit, to make you good, obedient, gentle, kind, truth-speaking children, to keep you from being selfish, idle, greedy, passionate, cunning, or ill-tempered. You must tell Him all you are afraid of, all you feel, and all you wish to have for your soul. This is prayer.

And you need not be afraid of Him at all when you pray. He would like you to tell Him all in your own simple way, just as you tell your own mothers when you want anything. He loves children very much. He was once much displeased with His disciples because they prevented people bringing their children to Him. He said, "Suffer the little children to come unto Me, and forbid them not." And He is just the same now that He was then.

Dear children, I should like you all to be praying children, children who tell the Lord all your wants and are not afraid to speak to Him. Prayer is the surest way to seek Him, and without prayer your souls will never prosper. Never mind if your prayers seem very poor and weak. Only let them come from your hearts and the Lord hears them.

The Lord Jesus hears every prayer that is prayed to Him in earnest. The least prayer of a little child on earth is loud enough to be heard plainly in heaven above. Heaven seems to be a long way off, but you may be sure the very moment the prayer is spoken it is heard there. A little key will often open a great door. Prayer is a little key of that sort. It can open the door of heaven and take you up to the very throne of God Himself. Blessed are they who delight in prayer and call much upon God.

This, then, is the third way to seek the Lord Jesus Christ. You must seek Him in prayer.

Dear children, I have told you how to seek the Lord. Ask yourselves, each one of you, before you go any further, "Do I really seek Him?"

4. But our text tells us something about those who seek Jesus Christ. What is it? It

says they "shall find Him."

The Lord promises, "they that seek Me shall find Me." How sweet it is to hear that! Think how disagreeable it would be to seek and seek all our lives, and have our trouble for nothing and never find Him. But the Lord says, "They shall find Me."

Now I want to tell you what this "finding" means. We shall not see Him with our eyes, for He is sitting at God's right hand in heaven and not on earth; and yet we are told we shall find Him. How can this be? Let me tell you.

You will find the Lord's presence in your own hearts and minds. You will feel something within you, as if the Lord Jesus Christ was sitting by you, taking care of you, putting His arm around you, smiling upon you, and speaking kindly to you. Just as a blind person feels brighter and happier when the sun is shining pleasantly on him, though he cannot see it, so you and I, if we seek Jesus Christ in earnest, shall soon feel our hearts lighter and happier, and something within us will make us know that we have found Him.

Dear children, it is sweet and comfortable indeed when we feel that we have really found Jesus Christ. Oh, that you may never give up seeking till you have found Him! And you will find Him, I know, if you seek on, for He is not far off. He is very near everyone of us, waiting for us to call upon Him.

When you have found Him, you will feel as if you have a sure Friend in whom you can trust: a Friend who will always love you, always watch over you, always take care of you, always be good to you, and never fail you.

When you have found Him, you will feel as if you have gotten strength and power to walk in God's ways, strength to keep yourself from bad words and bad company, strength to do things which please God.

When you have found Him, you will feel as if you have a pleasant Comforter living in your heart. You will be far more happy, cheerful, and content than you were before. Little things will not put you out as they used to do. You will not be afraid of sickness, pain, or death.

Dear children, how delightful it will be to feel all this! Try, all of you, do try to find Jesus Christ.

5. And now there is only one thing more in our text that I want to talk to you about, only one little word. But that little word is so very important that I dare not pass it over. It is the word "early."

"They that seek Me early," the Lord Jesus Christ says, "they are those that shall find Me."

Dear children, that word "early" was meant particularly for you. Seeking Jesus Christ early means seeking Jesus Christ when you are quite young; and that is just what I want you all to do.

Children, the Lord sends a message to you this very day by my mouth: He would like you to begin seeking Him at once.

Now, remember, all of you, you cannot begin seeking Jesus too soon.

Seeking early is the safest way. Children may be young and healthy, but no children are too young and healthy to die. For death is very strong; death can soon make the healthiest of you pine away, and make your rosy cheeks pale and sickly. Death is very cruel; it does not care whom it takes away out of families, and it will not wait for anyone to get ready. Death will take you just when it pleases. I think as many young persons die as old ones. I see the names of as many young people as old on the gravestones.

Children, you would not like to die without having sought the Lord at all. Oh, remember, seeking early is the safest way! And then, besides this, seeking early is the happiest way. Surely, if it is so pleasant to have Jesus Christ for a Friend, the sooner you have Him for a Friend the better. You cannot think how happily a child's life goes on when his ways please the Lord! Everything seems bright and cheerful; lessons seem more easy and play seems more pleasant; friends seem more kind and trouble seems less troublesome; and everything in life seems more smooth. Dear children, I want you to enjoy all this. Then make haste and delay not to seek the Lord.

And, last of all, seeking early is the easiest way. When you and I have a great deal of work to do, you know there is nothing like beginning in good time. Now this is just what you should do about your souls: you should begin in good time to seek Him who alone can save them. People who have work to do that must be finished before dark take care to get up early in the morning. So should you do, dear children, in working about your souls. You should seek the Lord in the morning of life, and get your work done before the night of death comes when none can work. Every year you put it off you will find it harder work—more to be done and less time to do it. Every year you will find your hearts more stubborn, more unwilling to do what is right. Now they are like young trees, so soft and tender that by the Lord's help you may bend them any way. In a few years they will be like strong, thick trees, so tough and well-rooted that nothing but a mighty wind can shake them. Dear children, begin to seek the Lord at once. I want you to have as few difficulties as possible on your journey to heaven.

Consider these things. Consider them well and begin early to seek the Lord. It is the safest way, the happiest way, the easiest way. Try to be like Obadiah, who feared the Lord from his youth. Try to be like our blessed Lord Jesus Christ Himself, who grew up "in favor with God and man."

Think of the day when Jesus Christ shall come again to this world. He means to come again in the clouds of heaven, with power and great glory. He will come very suddenly, in an hour when no man thinks, like a thief in the night. He will gather together all who love Him and take them home to His Father's house to be forever happy. He will leave behind all the idle, wicked, and unbelieving persons who have not sought Him to be wretched and miserable forever.

Dear children, Jesus Christ might come very soon. We do not know how soon. How sad it would then be to see others taken up to heaven and ourselves left behind! How dreadful to feel, "I might have been taken up too, but I would not seek the Lord!"

Think too of the great day of judgment, when all of us shall stand before God and give account of our works. Some of the people who are saved will say then, "I never began to seek Jesus Christ till I was forty years old, and I wasted away more than half my life."

Others will say, "I never began to seek Him till I was twenty, and I wasted many years of my life."

But some will be able to say, "I sought the Lord when I was quite young. I can hardly remember the time when I did not try to love Him."

Dear children, how pleasant it will be for those people to think this! How sweet to feel that they gave the first days of their lives as well as the last to Jesus Christ! How glorious they will appear who have loved their Savior in the beginning of their time as well as in the end! May the Lord grant that many of you may be found among them. Oh, seek the Lord early; seek Him while He may be found.

And now, dear children, it is time for me to leave off and let you go. Perhaps I shall never see you all together again in this world. Indeed I am almost sure I shall not, but we shall all meet at the last day. I do hope you will think of what I have told you about Jesus Christ and your souls. Remember, I want you all to be happy children, and in order to be happy you must love Jesus Christ.

Little and Wise

"There be four things which are little upon the earth, but they are exceeding wise: The ants are a people not strong, yet they prepare their meat in the summer. The conies are but a feeble folk, yet make they their houses in the rocks. The locusts have no king, yet go they forth all of them by bands. The spider taketh hold with her hands, and is in kings' palaces." Proverbs 30:24–28

Dear children, I would like you all to be very wise. Wisdom is far better than money or fine clothes or grand houses or horses and carriages. People who are not wise seldom get on well. They are seldom happy. My best wish for any dear boys and girls that I love is that they may grow up very wise.

"But how are we to be wise?" some of you will ask. "What are we to do in order to get this wisdom, which you tell us is such a good thing?"

Dear children, if you would be wise you must pray to God to make you so. You must ask Him to put His Holy Spirit in your hearts and give you wisdom. This is one thing.

Besides this, you must read God's holy book, the Bible. There you will find out what true wisdom is. There you will see what kind of things wise people do. This is another thing.

And now let me talk to you about those five verses in the Bible which I have given you. They are verses which tell us about wisdom. I hope they will do you much good.

There you see that God tells you to learn a lesson of four little creatures—the ant, the coney, the locust, and the spider. He seems to say that they are all patterns of wisdom. They are all poor, little, weak things. An ant is a little creeping insect, that *everybody* knows. A coney is a little creature very much like a rabbit (some call it a badger). A locust is like a large grass-hopper. A spider is a thing that the least child needs not be afraid of. But God tells you that the ant, the coney, the locust, and the spider are very wise. Come then, dear children, and listen to me while I tell you something about them. Some of you are but little now, but here you see it is possible to be little and yet wise.

1. First of all, what are you to learn from the ants? You must learn of the little ants to take thought about time to come.

"The ants," says the Bible, "prepare their meat in the summer." God has made the ants so wise and thoughtful that they go about gathering food in the harvest time. They are not idle in the fine long days when the sun shines. They get all the grains of corn they can find and lay them up in their nests. And so, when frost and snow come, the ants are not starved. They lie snug in their nests and have plenty to eat.

The butterflies are much prettier to look

at than the ants. They have beautiful wings and make a much finer show. But the butterflies, poor things, are not as wise as the ants. They fly about among the flowers and enjoy themselves all summer. They never think of gathering food for the winter. But what happens when the winter comes? The poor butterflies all die while the ants stay alive.

And now, dear children, I want you each to learn wisdom from the ants. I want you, like them, to think of time to come.

You each have within you a soul that will live forever. Your body will die some time; your soul never will. And your soul needs thought and care as much as your body. It needs to have its sins pardoned; it needs grace to make it please God; it needs power to be good; it needs to have God for its best Friend in order to be happy.

And, dear children, the best time for seeking pardon, grace, and the friendship of God is the time of youth. Youth and childhood are your summer. Now you are strong and well; now you have plenty of time; now you have few cares and troubles to distract you. Now is the best time for laying up food for your souls.

Ah, my beloved children, you must remember that winter is before you! Old age is your winter. Your frost, snow, rain, and storms are all yet to come. Sorrow, pain, sickness, death, and judgment will all come with old age. Happy are those who get ready for it quickly. Happy are those who, like the ants, take thought for things to come!

Those are wise boys and girls who read their Bibles and learn many texts by heart. Those are wise boys and girls who pray God every day to give them His Holy Spirit. Those are wise who mind what their parents and teachers tell them and take pains to be good. Those are wise who dislike all bad ways and bad words and always tell the truth. Such boys and girls are like the little ants: they are laying up store against time to come.

Dear children, if you have not done so before, I hope you will begin to do so now. If you have done so, I hope you will keep on doing so, and do so more and more. Do not be like the foolish butterflies. Be like the ants. Think of time to come and be wise.

2. But let us now go on and see what you are to learn from the conies. You must learn from the little conies to have a place of safety to flee to in time of danger.

"The conies," says the Bible, "make their houses in the rocks." The conies are afraid of foxes, dogs, and cruel men who hunt and kill them. They are poor, weak things and are not strong enough to fight and take care of themselves. So what do they do? They make their holes among stones and rocks whenever they can. They go where men cannot dig them out. They go where dogs and foxes cannot follow them; and then when they see men, or dogs, or foxes coming they run away into those holes and are safe.

The hare can run much faster than the coney, for it has much longer legs. The stag is much bigger than the coney and has fine horns. But the hare and the stag have no holes to run into. They lie out on the open fields, and so when men come to hunt them with dogs and guns they are soon caught and killed. But the little coney has a hiding place to run to, and in this way he often escapes.

Now, dear children, I want you to learn wisdom from the little conies. I want you to have a place of safety for your souls.

Your souls have many enemies. You are in danger from many things which may do them harm. You have, each of you, a wicked heart within you. Have you not often found how hard it is to be good? You each have a terrible enemy, seeking to ruin you forever and take you to hell. That enemy is the devil. You cannot see him, but he is never far off. You are each living in a world where there are many bad people and few good ones. Dear children, all these things are against you.

You need the help of One who can keep you safe. You need a hiding place for your precious souls. You need a dear Friend who is able to save you from your evil hearts, from the devil and the bad example of wicked people. Listen to me and I will tell you about Him.

There is One who is able to keep your souls quite safe. His name is Jesus Christ. He is strong enough to save you, for He is God's own Son. He is willing to save you, for He came down from heaven and died upon the cross for your sakes. And He loves all children. He liked to have them with Him when He was upon earth. He took them up in His arms and blessed them.

Dear children, those boys and girls are wise who put their trust in Jesus Christ and ask Him to take care of their souls. Such boys and girls will be kept safe. Jesus Christ loves them. Jesus Christ will not let them come to harm. He will not allow the devil or wicked people to ruin their souls. Jesus is the true Rock for children to flee to. Boys and girls who trust Him will be cared for while they live and go to heaven when they die. Jesus is the true hiding place. Boys and girls who love Him will be safe and happy.

Dear children, I hope you will all try to have your souls kept safe. Do not put off asking the Lord Jesus Christ to take care of them. Do not say to yourselves, "Oh, we shall have plenty of time by and by." Who knows what may happen to you before long. Perhaps you may be sick and ill; perhaps you may lose all your kind friends and be left alone. Oh, go and pray to Jesus now! Be like the wise little conies. Get a safe hiding place for your soul.

3. Let us now see what you are to learn from the locusts. You must learn from the locusts to love one another, to keep together and help one another.

"The locusts," says the Bible, "have no king, yet go they forth all of them by bands." They have nobody over them to tell them what to do. They are poor, little, weak insects by themselves. One locust alone can do very little. The least boy or girl would kill a locust if he were to tread on it. It would be dead at once.

But the little locusts are so wise that they always keep together. They fly about in such numbers that you could not count them; you would think they were a black cloud. They do not quarrel with one another; they help each other; and in this way the locusts are able to do a very great deal. They make the farmers and gardeners quite afraid when they are seen coming. They eat up the grass and corn; they strip all the leaves off the trees, and this is because they help one another.

Dear children, I want you to learn from the little locusts always to love one another and never to quarrel. You should try to be kind and good-natured to other boys and girls. You should make it a rule never to be selfish, never to be spiteful, never to get into a passion, never to fight with one another. Boys and girls who do such things are not wise. They are more foolish than the locusts.

Dear children, quarreling is very wicked. It pleases the devil, for he is always trying to make people wicked like himself. It does not please God, for God is love. Selfishness and quarreling are most improper in Christian children. They should try to be like Christ. Christ was never selfish. He pleased not Himself.

Think what a great deal of good boys and girls might do if they would be like the locust and love one another. Think how useful they might be to their fathers and mothers; they might save them much trouble and help in many little ways. Think what a great deal of money they might collect to help the missionaries to the poor heathen. If every child in England were to collect sixpence a year by asking people for farthings to help the missionaries, it would be a very great sum. Think, above all, what good boys and girls might do if they agreed to pray for one another. How happy they would soon be! Such prayers would be heard.

Dear children, as long as you live, love one another. Try to be of one mind. Have nothing to do with quarreling and fighting —hate it and think it a great sin. You ought to agree together far better than the little locusts. They have no king to teach them. You have a King who has promised His Spirit to teach you, and that King is Christ. Oh, be wise like the locusts and love one another.

4. And now, last of all, let us see what you are to learn from the spider. You must learn from the spider not to give up trying to be good because of a little trouble.

"The spider," says the Bible, "taketh hold with her hands, and is in kings' palaces." The spider is a poor, little, feeble thing, you all know. But the spider takes great pains in making her web. The spider creeps into grand houses and climbs to the top of the finest rooms, and there she spins her web. There seems to be no keeping her out. The servants come and brush the web away, and the spider sets to work at once and makes it again new. No insect is so persevering as the spider. She does her work over and over again. She will not give up.

I remember a story of a great king who got back his kingdom by taking an example from a spider. This poor man had been driven away from his kingdom, like David, by wicked rebels. He had tried often to get his kingdom back. He had fought many battles, but had always been beaten. At last he began to think it was no use; he would give up and fight no more. It happened at that time that he was lying awake in bed very early one summer's morning when he saw a spider at work. The spider was trying to make a thread from one side of the room to the other. Twelve times she tried in vain. Twelve times the thread broke and she fell to the ground. Twelve times she got up and tried again. But she did not give up. She persevered, and the thirteenth time she succeeded. Now when the king saw that he said to himself, "Why should not I persevere too in trying to get back my kingdom? Why should not I succeed at last, though I have so often failed?" He did try again, and he succeeded. He conquered his cruel enemies and got back his kingdom. Dear children, this king's name was Robert Bruce. He got back his kingdom in Scotland by copying the spider.

Now I want you to make the spider your pattern for your souls. I want you, like the spider, to persevere in sticking to what is good. I would like you to determine that you will never give up. I want you to keep on trying not to do what is evil, and trying always to do what is good and pleasing to God.

Ah, dear children, it is a wicked world, I am sorry to say; and there are many who will try hard to make you wicked as you grow up! The devil will try hard to make you forget God. Bad men and women will tell you there is no need for you to be so good.

I beg you not to give way. I beseech you to persevere. Keep on praying every day; keep on reading your Bibles regularly; keep on regularly going to church on Sunday. Alas, there are many boys and girls who give up everything that is good as soon as they leave school! While they are at school they use their Bibles, their hymnbooks, and their prayerbooks. When they stop going to school, they stop using all their books too. They often get into bad company; they often take up bad ways; they often go idling about all Sunday; they seem to forget all that has been taught them. Alas, this is not persevering! This is being more foolish than the little spider. It is wicked and unwise.

Dear children, there is a glorious house in heaven where, I hope, I shall see some of you. There is a palace there belonging to

Jesus Christ, far finer than any palace on earth, in which all Jesus Christ's people shall live and be happy forever and ever. Dear children, I hope I shall see many of you there.

But, remember, if you and I are to meet in this glorious palace you must persevere and take pains about your souls. You must pray heartily. You must read your Bibles regularly. You must fight against sin daily. You must say, when bad people entice you to do wrong, "I will not give up my religion. I will try to please Christ." Oh, let the little spider be your pattern all your lives! Persevere and be wise.

And now, dear children, I will finish by asking you to think of what I have been telling you. I have told you of four little creatures which are very wise—the ants, the conies, the locusts, and the spiders. I have shown you that the ants are a pattern of wisdom because they think of time to come. The conies are a pattern of wisdom because they make their houses in safe places. The locusts are a pattern of wisdom because they help one another. The spiders are a pattern of wisdom because they persevere. Dear children, I want you to be like them. Some of you may possibly never live to be men and women. But one thing you may be even now: you may be wise.

Be wise like the ants. Consider these two verses of the Bible and learn them by heart: "Remember thy Creator in the days of thy youth" (Ecclesiastes 12:1). "Prepare to meet thy God" (Amos 4:12).

Be wise like the conies. Consider these two verses of the Bible and learn them by heart: "Believe on the Lord Jesus Christ and thou shalt be saved" (Acts 16:31). "Thou art my hiding-place; thou shalt preserve me from trouble" (Psalm 32:7).

Be wise like the locusts. Consider these two verses of the Bible and learn them by heart: "By this shall all men know that ye are My disciples, if ye have love one towards another" (John 13:35). "He that loveth not his brother, whom he hath seen, how can he love God, whom he hath not seen?" (1 John 4:20).

Be wise like the spiders. Consider these words of the Bible and learn them by heart: "Ask, and it shall be given you; seek, and ye shall find" (Matthew 7:7). "Let us lay aside every weight, and the sin which doth so easily beset us; and let us run with patience the race that is set before us, looking unto Jesus" (Hebrews 12:1–2).

Dear children, think on these things. This is the way to be both happy and wise. Never forget what God says in the Bible: "Better is a poor and wise child than an old and foolish king" (Ecclesiastes 4:13). "The wise shall inherit glory" (Proverbs 3:35).

The Two Bears

"He went up from thence unto Bethel; and as he was going up by the way, there came forth little children out of the city, and mocked him, and said unto him, Go up, thou bald head; go up, thou bald head. And he turned back, and looked on them, and cursed them in the name of the Lord. And there came forth two she-bears out of the wood, and tore forty and two children of them." 2 Kings 2:23–24

Dear children, did you ever see a bear? Perhaps not. There are no wild bears in this country now. There are some that are kept tied up in wild beast shows or are carried about in cages. But there are none loose in the woods and fields. So perhaps you never saw a bear.

A bear is a large, shaggy, savage, wild beast with great teeth and claws, and is

51

very strong. It will kill sheep, lambs, calves, and goats and eat them. When it is very hungry it will attack men, women, or children and tear them to pieces. She-bears that have little cubs are particularly fierce and cruel. How thankful we ought to be that we can walk about in England without fear of being caught by a bear!

Now I am going to tell you a story about a good man, two bears, and some children. It is a story out of the Bible, and so you may be sure that it is all true. Stories in other books are often only "make-believe," and tell us things that never really happened. Stories out of the Bible, you must always remember, are true, every word. Never forget that!

Once upon a time, about twenty-seven hundred years ago, there lived a good man whose name was Elisha. He was at first a servant to a famous prophet of God named Elijah. After Elijah was taken up to heaven in a chariot of fire, Elisha was appointed to be prophet in his place. From that time to his death he was a very great man, and a very useful man. He did many miracles. He used to go up and down the land of Israel, teaching people how to serve God, and reproving sinners. In some places he kept up schools called "schools of the prophets." In this way he became famous all over the country. All the people knew Elisha, and all good people loved him.

One day, not long after Elijah had been taken up to heaven, Elisha went to a place called Bethel where there was a school. I dare say he went to see how the school was getting on, and whether it was doing any good. All schools need looking after and examining, and it does them good to be examined. It is only bad boys and girls who dislike being asked what they have learned.

Now as this good old man Elisha got near Bethel, a very sad thing happened. A great number of little children came out of the town and behaved extremely poorly. They began to mock Elisha and call him names. Instead of respecting him, and bowing to him, like good children, they made fun of him and said silly things. "Go up, thou bald head," they cried, "go up, thou bald head." They called him "bald head," I have no doubt, because the good prophet was old and had no hair on his head. They said "Go up," I suspect, because his master Elijah had lately gone up to heaven, as everybody knew. And they meant that Elisha had better go away after his master, and not trouble them any more with his teaching. It was as much as saying, "Be off and begone! It is high time for you to go up, as well as your master."

Just think for a moment how wicked these children were! They lived in a town where they might have learned better things. There was a school of prophets at Bethel. But I am afraid they had not used their opportunities, and had loved play better than lessons. They had no business to mock Elisha and treat him so badly. He had done them no harm, and had never been unkind to them. He was a good man, and one who was their best friend. Above all, they ought not to have said, "Go up, and get away." They ought rather to have said, "Stay with us, and teach us the way to heaven." Truly it is sad to see to what lengths of wickedness even little children may go. It is sad to see how corrupt boys and girls may become, and what naughty things they will say, even when they live close to a school!

But what did Elisha do when these children behaved so ill? We are told that he "turned back and looked on them" with sorrow and displeasure. They had probably often done the same thing before. It had become a habit with them which could not be cured. The time had come when they must be punished. And then we are told that "he cursed them in the name of the Lord." That does not mean, you may be sure, that Elisha flew into a passion and swore at the children, as some bad old men might have done. He was not the man to do that! It only means that he solemnly pronounced God's anger and displeasure against them. He gravely told them "in the name of the Lord" that God would certainly punish them, and that it was his duty, as God's servant, to say so. No, indeed, Elisha did not speak in passion or ill temper. The judge at the court is not angry with the prisoner when he sentences him to be put in prison. When Elisha pronounced God's curse on these wicked children, he did it as God's appointed servant, firmly and faithfully, but in sorrow. God told him, no doubt, what to do, and like an obedient servant he did it.

And what happened as soon as Elisha had spoken? At once there came forth out of a wood close by two she-bears, which rushed upon these wicked children, tearing and killing all they caught. Think what an awful surprise that must have been! How dreadfully frightened these children must have felt! What running, and screaming, and tumbling over one another, and crying for help there must have been! How sorry and ashamed of themselves they must have felt! But with many it was too late. Before they could get within the walls of Bethel the bears had caught and killed no less than forty-two children. Forty-two little boys and girls never came home to Bethel alive that night. Forty-two little suppers were not eaten! Forty-two little beds were not slept in! Forty-two little funerals took place next day! Many children, I cannot help hoping, got home safely and were not hurt. But I am sure they would never forget what they had seen. They would remember the two bears as long as they lived.

Now, dear children, this is a sad story. But it is a very useful and instructive one. Like everything else in the Bible it was written for your good. It teaches lessons which boys and girls ought never to forget. Let me tell you what those lessons are.

1. Learn that God takes notice of what children do. He took notice of the "little children" at Bethel and punished them for their wickedness. Remember, I beg you,

that God is not altered. He is still the same. He is taking notice of you every day.

I believe some people fancy that it does not matter how children behave, because God only notices grown-up men and women. This is a very great mistake. The eyes of God are upon boys and girls, and He marks all they do. When they do right He is pleased and when they do wrong He is displeased. Dear children, never forget this.

Let no one make you think that you are too young to serve God, and that you may safely wait till you are men and women. This is not true. It is never too soon to take up religion. As soon as you know right from wrong, you are old enough to begin taking the right way. As soon as you are old enough to be punished for doing wrong, you are old enough to give your heart to God and follow Christ. The child who is old enough to be chastised for swearing and telling lies is not too young to be taught to pray and read the Bible. The child who is big enough to displease God is also big enough to please Him. The child who is old enough to be tempted by the devil is not too young to have the grace of the Holy Spirit in his heart.

Children, however little and young you are, God is always noticing you. He notices how you behave at home, how you behave at school, and how you behave at play. He notices whether you say your prayers or not, and how you say them. He notices whether you mind what your mother tells you and how you act when you are out of your mother's sight. He notices whether you are greedy or selfish or cross or tell lies or take what is not your own. In short, there is nothing about children that God does not notice.

I read in the Bible that when little Ishmael was almost dead with thirst in the wilderness, "God heard the voice of the lad" (Genesis 21:17). Mark it, He listened to the child's prayer. I read that when Samuel was only a little boy, God spoke to him (1 Samuel 3:10). I read that when Abijah, the child of Jeroboam, was sick and dying, God said by the mouth of His prophet, "There is some good thing found in him toward the Lord God of Israel" (1 Kings 14:13). Children, these things were written for your learning.

Now I will give you a piece of advice. Say to yourselves every morning when you get up, "God sees me. Let me live as in God's sight." God is always looking at what you do, and hearing what you say. All is put down in His great books, and all must be reckoned for at the last day. It is written in the Bible, "Even a child is known by his doings" (Proverbs 20:11).

2. Learn that it is very wrong to mock good people and despise religion. The little children of Bethel mocked Elisha and called him "bald head." For doing so they were terribly punished.

Dear children, as long as you live make it a rule never to laugh at religion or mock anybody who is religious. This is one of the wickedest things you can do. It is pleasant to see boys and girls merry and happy. Youth is the time for laughter and merriment. But take care never to laugh at anything belonging to God. Whatever you laugh at, do not laugh at religion.

Some boys and girls, I am sorry to say, are very thoughtless about this. They think it is clever to make fun of those who read their Bibles, say their prayers, keep their Sundays properly, and attend to what is said at church. They laugh at other boys and girls who mind what their mothers say and try to corrupt them. Some, indeed, are so wicked that when they see other children trying to do what pleases God, they point their fingers at them and cry, "There goes a little *saint*."

Now, all this is very wrong and offends God exceedingly. There sits One in heaven who sees these wicked children, and when He sees them He is greatly displeased. We cannot wonder if such children come to trouble or turn out badly. All who despise God's people despise God Himself. It is written, "Them that honor Me I will honor, and they that despise Me shall be lightly esteemed" (1 Samuel 2:30).

I read in the Bible that Ishmael was turned out of Abraham's house because he mocked his little brother, Isaac. Saint Paul tells us that "he persecuted him" (Genesis 21:9; Galatians 4:29). At the time when Ishmael did this, he was only a boy. But, boy as he was, he was old enough to offend God by mocking, and to bring himself and his mother into great trouble.

Dear children, some of you perhaps have good fathers and mothers who tell you to read your Bibles and say your prayers. I hope that you never laugh at them behind their backs and mock what they tell you about religion. Be sure that, if you do this, you commit a great sin. It is written, "The eye that mocketh at his father, and despiseth to obey his mother, the ravens of the valley shall pick it out, and the young eagles shall eat it" (Proverbs 30:17).

3. Learn in the last place that sin is sure to bring sorrow at last. It brought wounds and death on the little children of Bethel. It brought weeping and crying to the homes of their parents. If these wicked boys and girls had not displeased God, they would not have been torn by the bears.

Dear children, as long as you live, you will always see the same thing. Those who will have their own way and run into sin are sure, sooner or later, to find themselves in trouble. This trouble may not come at once. It may even be kept off for many long years. But sooner or later it is sure to come. There is a dreadful hell at last, and those who will go on sowing sin are sure at last to reap sorrow.

Adam and Eve ate the forbidden fruit in Eden. What was the consequence? Sorrow. They were cast out of the garden with shame.

The people before the flood went on

eating and drinking and despising Noah's advice about the flood. And what was the consequence? Sorrow. The flood came and they were all drowned.

The people of Sodom and Gomorrah went on sinning in spite of Lot's warnings. And what was the consequence? Sorrow. The fire fell from heaven and they were all burned.

Esau would have the mess of pottage, and despised his birthright. And what was the consequence? Sorrow. He sought it afterward too late, with many tears.

The children of Israel would not obey God's command and go up into the land of Canaan when He commanded them. And what was the consequence? Sorrow. They wandered forty years in the wilderness.

Achan, when Jericho was taken, would not obey the command of Joshua, but took money and hid it under his tent. And what was the consequence? Sorrow. He was found out and publicly stoned.

Judas Iscariot, who was one of the twelve

Apostles, would not give his whole heart to Christ, but coveted money and betrayed his Master. And what was the consequence? Sorrow. The money did him no good. It did not make him happy, and he went out and hanged himself.

Ananias and Sapphira told a great lie to Peter and the Apostles in order to be thought good, and yet keep hold of their riches at the same time. And what was the consequence? Sorrow. They were both struck dead in one day.

Dear children, remember these things to the end of your lives. The wages of sin is death. The fruit of sin at last is trouble. Those who tell lies or steal or get drunk or break the Sabbath may not suffer for it at first. But their sin will find them out. Sooner or later, in this world or the next, those who sow sin, like the children of Bethel, are sure to reap sorrow. The way of transgressors is hard.

And now I will finish all I have been

saying with three parting counsels. Consider them well, and lay them to heart.

1. Settle it in your minds that the way to be happy is to be really good in the sight of God. If you will have your own way and follow sin, you are sure to have trouble and sorrow.

2. If you want to be really good, ask the Lord Jesus Christ to make you good and put His Spirit into your hearts. You cannot make yourselves good, I know. Your hearts are too weak, and the world and the devil are too strong. But Jesus Christ can make you good, and He is ready and willing to do so. He can give you new hearts and the power to overcome sin. Then take Jesus Christ for your Shepherd and Friend. Cast your souls upon Him.

Jesus, who died on the cross to save us, has a special care for little children. He says, "I love them that love Me, and those that seek Me early shall find Me" (Proverbs 8:17).

"Suffer the little children to come unto

Me, and forbid them not, for of such is the kingdom of God" (Matthew 19:14).

3. In the last place, if you want to be kept from the evil that is in the world, remember daily that God sees you, and live as in God's sight. Never mock good people or make fun of religion. Love those most who love God most, and choose for your friends those who are God's friends. Hate sin of all sorts. When sinners entice you, do not consent. Abhor that which is evil. Cleave to that which is good.

Dear children, if you live in this way, God will bless you, and you will find at last that you have "chosen the good part which cannot be taken from you" (Luke 10:42).

Remember these things and you will have learned something from "The Two Bears."

Children Walking in Truth

"I rejoiced greatly that I found of thy children walking in truth." 2 John 4

Beloved children, the book from which my text is taken is the shortest in the Bible. Look at it when you go home and you will find it so. It has only thirteen verses. But, short as it is, it is full of important things, and I think the verse I have just read is one of them.

This book is an epistle, or letter, written by the Apostle John. He wrote it to a good Christian lady whom he knew. This lady had children, and some of them were the children spoken of in the text.

It seems that John found some of this good lady's children at a place where he happened to go; and you see how well he found them behaving. He was able to write a good report of them to their mother, and that is the report of our text: "I rejoiced greatly that I found of thy children walking in truth."

Now, dear children, there are only two things I want to tell you about out of this text. Some of you perhaps are thinking this very minute: "What does walking in truth mean?" Others perhaps are thinking: "Why did John rejoice so greatly?"

I shall try to answer these two questions. First, I shall try to show you when it can be said that children walk in truth. Second, I shall try to show you what the reasons were that made the Apostle John rejoice so greatly.

Dear children, let me ask you all one favor. I shall not keep you long. Come and listen to what I have to tell you. May the Holy Spirit open all your hearts and bless what I say.

I told you I would first try to show you when it can be said that children walk in truth. Let me set about it at once.

What does "walking" mean here? You

must not think it means walking on your feet, like you have walked here tonight. It means, rather, our way of behaving our-selves—our way of living and going on. And shall I tell you why the Bible calls this "walking"? It calls it so because a man's life is just like a journey. From the time of our birth to the time of our death we are always traveling and moving on. Life is a journey from the cradle to the grave, and a person's manner of living is, on that account, often called his "walk."

But what does "walking in truth" mean? It means walking in the ways of true Bible religion, and not in the bad ways of this evil world. The world, I am sorry to tell you, is full of false notions and untruths, and *especially* full of untruths about religion. They all come from our great enemy, the devil. The devil deceived Adam and Eve in Eden, and made them sin by telling them an untruth. He told them they would not die if they ate the forbidden fruit, and that was untrue. And the devil is always at the same work now. He is always trying to make men, women, and children have false notions about God and about religion. He persuades them to believe that what is really evil is good, and what is really good is evil—that God's service is not pleasant, and that sin will do them no great harm. And, I grieve to say, vast numbers of people are deceived by him and believe these untruths.

But those persons who walk in truth are very different. They pay no attention to the false notions there are in the world about religion. They follow the true way which God shows us in the Bible. Whatever others may do, their chief desire is to please God and be His true servants. Now this was the character of the children spoken of in the text. John writes home to their mother and says, "I found them walking in truth."

Dear children, would you not like to know whether you are walking in truth yourselves? Would you like to know the marks by which you may find it out? Listen, every one of you, while I try to set these marks before you in order. Let every boy and girl come and hear what I am going to say.

1. I tell you, then, for one thing, that children who walk in truth know the truth about sin.

What is sin? To break any command of God is sin. To do anything that God says ought not to be done is sin. God is very holy and very pure, and every sin that is sinned displeases Him exceedingly. But, in spite of all this, most people in the world, both old and young, think very little about sin. Some try to make out that they are not great sinners, and do not often break God's commandments. Others say that sin is not so terrible a thing after all, and that God is not so particular and strict as ministers say He is. These are two great and dangerous mistakes.

Children who walk in truth think very differently. They have no such proud and high feelings. They feel themselves full of sin, and it grieves and humbles them. They believe that sin is the abominable thing which God hates. They look upon sin as their greatest enemy and plague. They hate it more than anything on earth. There is nothing they so heartily desire to be free from as sin.

Dear children, there is the first mark of walking in truth. Look at it. Think of it. Do you hate sin?

2. I tell you for another thing that children who walk in truth love the true Savior of sinners and follow Him.

There are few men and women who do not feel they need in some way to be saved. They feel that after death comes the judgment, and from that awful judgment they would like to be saved.

But, alas! Few of them will see that the Bible says there is only one Savior, even Jesus Christ; and few go to Jesus Christ and ask Him to save them. They trust rather in their own prayers or their own repentance, or their own church-going or their own regular attendance at sacrament or their own goodness or something of the kind. But these things, although useful in their place, cannot save any one soul from hell. These are false ways of salvation. They cannot put away sin. They are not Christ.

Nothing can save you or me but Jesus Christ, who died for sinners on the cross. Those only who trust entirely in Him have their sins forgiven and will go to heaven. These alone will find they have an Almighty Friend in the day of judgment. This is the true way to be saved.

Children who walk in truth have learned all this, and if you ask them what they put their trust in they will answer, "Nothing but Christ." They remember His gracious words: "Suffer the little children to come unto Me, and forbid them not." They try to follow Jesus as the lambs follow the good shepherd. And they love Him because they read in the Bible that He loved them and gave Himself for them. Little children, there is the second mark of walking in truth. Look at it. Think of it. Do you love Christ?

3. I tell you that children who walk in truth serve God with a true heart.

I dare say you know it is very possible to serve God with outward service only. Many do so. They will put on a grave face and pretend to be serious while they do not feel it. They will say beautiful prayers with their lips and yet not mean what they say. They will sit in their places at church every Sunday and yet be thinking of other things all the time—and such service is outward service and very wrong.

Bad children, I am sorry to say, are often guilty of this sin. They will say their prayers regularly, when their parents *make* them, but not otherwise. They will seem to pay attention in church when the master's eye is upon them, but not at other times. Their hearts are far away.

Children who walk in truth are not so. They have another spirit in them. Their desire is to be honest in all they do with God, and to worship Him in spirit and in truth. When they pray, they try to be in earnest and mean all the words they say. When they go to church they try to be really serious and to give their minds to what they hear. And it is one of their chief troubles that they cannot serve God more heartily than they do.

Little children, there is the third mark of walking in truth. Look at it. Think of it. Is your heart false or true?

4. I tell you, for a last thing, that children who walk in truth really try to do things that are right and true in the sight of God.

God has told us very plainly what He thinks is right. Nobody can mistake this who reads the Bible with an honest heart. But it is sad to see how few men and women care for pleasing God. Many break His commandments continually and seem to think nothing of it. Some will tell lies, and swear and quarrel and cheat and steal. Others use bad words, break the Sabbath, never pray to God at all, and never read their Bibles. Others are unkind to their relations, or idle or gluttonous or bad-tempered or selfish. And all these things, whatever people may choose to think, are very wicked and displeasing to a holy God.

Children who walk in truth are always trying to keep clear of bad ways. They take no pleasure in sinful things of any kind, and they dislike the company of those who do them. Their great wish is to be like Jesus: holy, harmless, and separate from sinners. They endeavor to be kind, gentle, obliging, obedient, honest, truthful, and good in all their ways. It grieves them that they are not more holy than they are.

Little children, this is the last mark I shall give you of walking in truth. Look at it. Think of it. Are your doings right or wrong?

Children, you have now heard some marks of walking in truth. I have tried to set them plainly before you. I hope you have understood them. Knowing the truth about sin; loving the true Savior, Jesus Christ; serving God with a true heart; doing the things that are true and right in the sight of God—there they are, all four together. Think about them, I entreat you, and each ask yourself this question: "What am I doing at this very time; am I walking in truth?"

I dare be sure that many boys and girls here know well what answer they ought to give. And God knows too, for He sees your hearts as plainly as I see your faces this minute. Children, the all-seeing God sends you a question this night by my mouth. He says, "Are you walking in truth?"

Why should you not? Thousands of dear children have walked in truth already and found it pleasant. The way is trodden by many little feet of children before your own. Thousands of boys and girls are walking in truth at this moment, and there is yet room for more. Dear children, think this night: "Why should not you?"

And now I will go on to the second thing of which I promised to speak.

I said I would try to show you some of the reasons why John rejoiced to find this lady's children walking in truth. Let me set about it. The text says, "I rejoice greatly." Now why did he rejoice? There must have been some good reasons. John was not a man to rejoice without cause. Listen, dear children, and you shall hear what those reasons were.

1. For one thing, John rejoiced because he was a good man himself.

All good people like to see others walking in truth as well as themselves. I dare say you have heard how the angels in heaven rejoice when they see one sinner repenting. Some of you, no doubt, have read it in the fifteenth chapter of Luke. Well, good people are like the angels in this; they are full of love and compassion, and when they see anyone turning away from sin and doing what is right, it makes them feel happy.

Good people find walking in truth so pleasant that they would like everybody else to walk in truth too. They do not wish to keep all this pleasantness to themselves and go to heaven alone. They want to see all about them loving Jesus Christ and obeying Him—all their relations, all their neighbors, all their old friends, all their young ones—indeed, all the world. The more people they see walking in truth, the better they are pleased.

Children, John was a good man, and full of love for souls; and this was one reason why he rejoiced.

2. John rejoiced because it is very uncommon to see children walking in truth.

Dear children, I am very sorry to tell you, there are many bad boys and girls in the world. Too many are careless, thoughtless, self-willed, and disobedient. Nobody can rejoice over them. I hear many fathers and mothers complaining about this.

I hear many schoolmasters and school-mistresses speak of it. I am afraid it is quite true.

There are many children who will not give their minds to anything that is good. They will not do what they are bid. They like to be idle and have their own way. They love playing better than learning. They do things which God says are wicked and wrong, and they are not ashamed. All this is very sad to see.

John, you may be sure, had found this out, for he was an aged man as well as an Apostle, and had seen many things. He knew that even the children of good people sometimes turn out very badly. I dare say he remembered Jacob and David and all the sorrow their families caused them. And no doubt he knew what Solomon says in the Proverbs 22:15: "Foolishness is bound in the heart of a child."

When, therefore, John saw this lady's children not turning out bad like others, but walking in the way they should go, he might well feel it was a special mercy. I do not at all wonder that he greatly rejoiced.

3. John rejoiced because he knew that walking in truth would make these children really happy in this life.

John was not one of those foolish persons who do not like much religion, and fancy it makes people unhappy. John knew that the more true religion people have the more happy they are.

John knew that life is always full of care and trouble, and that the only way to get through life comfortably is to be a real follower and servant of Christ.

Dear children, remember what I say this night: If ever you would be happy in this evil world, you must give your hearts to Jesus Christ and follow Him. Give Him the entire charge of your souls and ask Him to be your Savior and your God; and then you will be happy. Have no will of your own and only try to please Him; and then your life will be pleasant.

Trust all to Christ and He will undertake

to manage all that concerns your soul.
Trust in Him at all times. Trust in Him in
every condition—in sickness and in health,
in youth and in age, in poverty and in
plenty, in sorrow and in joy. Trust in Him
and He will be a Shepherd to watch over
you—a Guide to lead you, a King to protect
you, a Friend to help you in time of need.
Trust in Him, and He says Himself, "I will
never leave thee nor forsake thee"
(Hebrews 13:8). He will put His Spirit into
you and give you a new heart. He will give
you power to become a true child of God.
He will give you grace to keep down bad
tempers, to no longer be selfish, to love
others as yourself. He will make your cares
more light and your work more easy. He
will comfort you in time of trouble. Christ
can make those happy who trust in Him.
Christ died to save them, and Christ ever
lives to give them peace.

Dear children, John was well aware of
these things. He had learned them by
experience. He saw this lady's children

likely to be happy in this world, and no wonder he rejoiced!

4. Last, John rejoiced because he knew that walking in truth in the life that now is would lead to glory and honor in the life to come.

The life to come is the life we should all think most of. Many people seem only to care for what happens to them in this life. But they are sadly mistaken. This life is very short; it will soon be over. The oldest man will tell you it seems only a few years since he was a child. The life to come is the life of real importance; it will have no end. It will either be never-ending happiness or never-ending pain. Oh, what a serious thought that is!

Children, I do not doubt that John was thinking of the life to come when he rejoiced. Our Lord Jesus Christ had often told him of the glorious rewards prepared for those who walk in truth. John thought of the rewards laid up in heaven for these children and was glad.

I do not doubt that John looked forward in his heart to that day when Jesus shall come again. I dare say he saw in his mind's eye these dear children clothed in robes white as snow, having golden crowns on their heads, standing at Jesus Christ's right hand, enjoying pleasures for evermore. He saw them and their beloved mother meeting again in heaven—meeting in that blessed place where parting and sorrow shall be known no more.

Dear children, these must have been sweet and pleasant thoughts. I do not wonder that John rejoiced.

And now I have finished what I have to say about our text. I have done what I promised. I have told you what it is to walk in truth. That is one thing. I have told you why John rejoiced so much to find this lady's children walking in truth. That is another. Let me now wind up all by saying something which, by God's help, may fasten this sermon in your minds. Alas, how many sermons are forgotten! I want this sermon to stick in your hearts and do good.

Ask yourselves, then, everyone, "Would John, if he knew me at this time, rejoice over me? Would John be pleased if he saw my ways and my behavior, or would he look sorrowful and grave?"

O children, children, do not neglect this question. This is no light matter. It may be your life. No wise man will ever rejoice over bad children. They may be clean and pretty, and have fine clothes and look well outwardly, but a wise man will only feel sad when he sees them. He will feel they are wrong inwardly—they do not have new hearts; they are not going to heaven. Believe me, it is far better to be good than to be pretty. It is far better to have grace in your hearts than to have much money in your pockets or fine clothes on your backs. None but children who love Christ are the children who make a wise man's heart rejoice.

Beloved children, hear the last words I have to say to you. I give you all an invitation from Christ, my Master. In His name I say to you, "Come and walk in truth."

This is the way to gladden the hearts of your parents and relations. This is the one thing above all others which will please your ministers and teachers. You little know how happy you make us when you try to walk in truth. Then we feel that all is well, though we die and leave you behind us in this evil world. Then we feel that your souls are safe, though we are called away and can help you and teach you no more. Then we feel that you are in the right way to be happy, and that you are prepared for troubles, however many may come upon you. For we know that walking in truth gives peace now, and we are sure that it leads to glory hereafter.

Come, then, this night, and begin to walk in truth. The devil will try to make you think it is too hard—that you cannot do it.

Believe him not; he is a liar! He wants to do you harm. Only trust in Christ and follow Him; you will soon say His way is a way of pleasantness and a path of peace. Only pray for the Holy Spirit to come into your heart and you will soon feel strong. He can guide you into all truth. Only read the Bible regularly and you will soon be made wise unto salvation. The Bible is the word of truth. Read and pray; pray and read. Begin these habits and keep them up. Do these things and, before long, you will not say it is impossible to walk in truth. But come; come at once.

Children, I find Jesus Christ saying, in the third chapter of Revelation, "Behold, I stand at the door and knock." Who knows but this may have been going on tonight? Who knows but Jesus may have been knocking at some of your hearts all through this sermon? If it is so, do not keep Him waiting any longer. If it is so, go to Him this night on your knees in prayer; go to Him and ask Him at once to come in.

Ask Jesus to come and dwell in your heart, and take care of it as His own. Ask Him to put your name in His book of life. Ask Him to enable you to walk in truth.

Oh, think how many children in the world have never been invited as you are! How many boys and girls have never had the chance of being saved that you enjoy; how many, perhaps, would leap for joy, and walk in truth at once if they were invited. Beloved children, take care. You, at least, cannot say you were not invited. Jesus invites you. The Bible invites you. I, the servant of Christ, invite you all tonight. Oh, come to Christ! Come and be happy. Come and walk in truth.

Little Things

My dear children, I have been asked to speak to the boys and girls who collect for the children's home known as the "Bird's Nest." I must begin by telling you that it is a very hard thing to do. I must get you all to help me. How can you help me? You can help me by being as quiet and attentive as you can, by sitting as still as you can, and by opening your ears as wide as you can.

Children, what is the first thing we want to do for the boys and girls in the "Bird's Nest"? I will tell you. Our great work is to help them to get to heaven. We want their souls to be saved by faith in the Lord Jesus Christ. We want them to be washed in Jesus' blood, clothed in His robe of righteousness, and made partakers of His grace. We want them to grow up holy, praying, Bible-reading, God-fearing men and women.

But some people may say, "What have boys and girls to do with this 'Bird's Nest'? Why not leave it to grown people to get all the money? They are better able to do it. Boys and girls should not have anything to do with it."

Why, dear boys and girls, there are no persons in the world who are so bound to work for the Lord Jesus Christ and the souls of people as children. There are none who ought to try so much to make known the gospel of Jesus Christ as children. Do you know what children come to in heathen lands? Here in this happy Christian country, when boys and girls are born, there is great joy and pleasure. On the contrary, it is a very common thing in heathen lands to kill the little child, to bury it alive or strangle it or starve it to death. Is it not very shocking? But these poor heathens know no better.

You have heard of the South Sea Islands. Look at the map of the world. Those little black dots to the left of South America are

the South Sea Islands. Well, these islands,
a few years ago, were full of idolaters. The
poor people there bowed down to sticks and
stones and knew nothing of the Lord Jesus
Christ. Kind missionaries went and told
them of Christ and salvation by Him. God
blessed their work, and many of the poor
heathens were converted; and many of
these heathen islands have now become
Christian islands. After they were converted, many of the people said, "We wish
we had heard these things before! If you
had only told us these things long ago, we
would never have done the wicked things
we did." And at one of these islands a
woman got up after a missionary meeting,
and said, "O sir, if I had only heard these
things before! I had nineteen little children,
and have murdered every one of them!
Because I knew nothing of the Bible, I
didn't care for my dear children. Oh, that I
had known long ago about Jesus Christ and
this blessed Bible, and about the way to
heaven!"

I always say that women, children, and the poor ought to do more for the gospel than any others in the world. It brings them so many blessings.

But now comes the question, What can *you* do? Many people will say, "Well, what can these little boys and girls do? What is the use of such little help as they can give to the 'Bird's Nest'?" O my dear children, who can tell the power of "littles"? The power of "littles" is very wonderful! No one knows what can be done by a "little" and a "little" and a "little."

Did you ever think about Noah's Ark? Did you ever think what a large thing Noah's Ark must have been? Just think of Noah having to make a vessel big enough to hold all the beasts and all the birds. How do you think the ark was made? It was not done all at once. Oh, no! It was made plank by plank and piece by piece, by little and little. Perhaps you would have said, if you had seen Noah at his work, "Oh, what's the use of that little piece, such a bit?" or,

"What's the use of that one plank?" Children, little by little is that which makes a large thing at last. So we want as many little things as we can get for the "Bird's Nest," and, joined together, they will make the whole of what we want.

God says in Zechariah 4:10, "Who hath despised the day of small things?" There is also a text spoken by our Lord Jesus Christ about little things. "He that is faithful in that which is least is faithful also in much; and he that is unjust in the least is unjust also in much." The real Christian must be faithful in little things as well as in great things.

Let me tell you a story of a man who knew the value of little things. This man became one of the most important people in the city of Paris. You know Paris is the capital city of France. Well, this man came to Paris when he was a boy, a little boy, not bigger than many of you. When he came there he wanted someone to find him something to do. Poor little fellow, he asked one man after another if they could give him some work. He was getting greatly discouraged, and quite tired of saying, "Please, sir, can you give me something to do?" and hearing the answer, "No, I have nothing for you to do; what can such a little fellow as you do?"

At last one day he went into a banker's house. There were a great many people standing in the office, so he went up to one of them and said, "Please, sir, can you find me something to do?"

"No, I cannot," was the answer.

As he went to the door to go away, he saw a pin upon the floor. He stooped down and picked it up and stuck it in his sleeve. The chief person in the office saw him do this and called him back. "Boy," said he, "what do you pick up that pin for? I don't want it, it would be of no value to me, but I want to know what made you pick it up."

"Well, sir," said the boy, "I will tell you. My mother told me never to waste little things, but always to take care of them!

She said, 'My son, if you will take care of little things, even of pins, you will always find some use for them.' I always like to do what my mother told me. I love my mother, and I always take care of little things."

These words struck the banker so much that he said, "My boy, come to me tomorrow morning." He did so, and the gentleman gave him a place in the bank. He turned out so steady and diligent that he soon rose from one thing to another, and in time he became the highest partner in the firm. And when he died he was the richest man in all Paris. His name was Laffitte.

Dear children, see what great results came from picking up a little pin. It showed character. It showed what the boy was. He was a boy who minded little things, and all his success in life afterwards he traced to this little circumstance. Little things are never to be despised. I always tell my own boys never to think lightly of everyday things. Oh, the importance of little habits!

Habits of reading, habits of prayer, habits at meals, little habits through the day—all are little things, but they make up the character, and are of the utmost importance. So, dear children, when people tell you there is no use in little helpers like you, don't mind them. By attending to little things, you will be able to do much for the "Bird's Nest."

Now what can you do?

1. Take a deep interest in the whole concern. Here are these boys and girls taught to be clean, taught to work, taught to behave well, taught to read the Bible, and taught to know the way to heaven. What a great work is this! What an honor to be a helper of it!

I know a clergyman who was once going to a missionary meeting. On the way he met a boy running in a very great hurry, so he stopped him and said, "My boy, why are you running so fast? What is the matter?"

"O sir," said the boy, "I am going to a

missionary meeting, and I must not lose a minute, for I am late."

"But what makes you in such a hurry about it? You are not wanted at it."

"Oh," said the boy, "I am part of the concern."

"How is that?" said the clergyman."

"Why, sir, it's a thing that I support, and I have a share in it myself." So off he ran to the meeting, and the clergyman followed. The report was read and the gentleman who read it out read that the total sum of money collected was so many pounds, so many shillings, and one penny.

"Oh," said the boy, "there goes my penny." So his giving the penny made him feel that he was part of the concern.

2. Always pray for the "Bird's Nest." If God's blessing is to be had, it must be sought. It is of great importance that all children should pray for God's blessing on every work they enter upon. One of our missionaries came home from India and

told us that, as he was going home one night, he passed by some trees and heard voices. He thought he would like to hear what was going on, and to his great joy he heard the voices of children praying. These heathen children were praying for a blessing upon the missions. He heard one child pray, "O Lord, I pray Thee to make my grandmother's ears longer."

I wonder if anyone here could tell what he meant by that prayer. I will tell you. He meant that, as his grandmother was a heathen, her heart was unchanged. She would not listen to what she was told about Christ, or she would pay no attention to what she heard. So her little grandson prayed that she might have longer ears in order to attend more to what the missionary said!

Dear children, can you not pray that God would make people's ears a great deal longer? People are told about the "Bird's Nest." You talk to them about the "Bird's Nest." You ask them to help you to give something to the "Bird's Nest." But you sometimes speak to them in vain. Their ears are so short that they will not listen, or do not understand what you mean. Could you not pray that the hearts of these people may be touched, so that more subscriptions may come in, that more active helpers may be raised up, and that God's work may go on faster and faster?

3. One thing more I will say. Let me beg you to help this cause by showing a missionary spirit at home. I should not like to hear of any boys or girls being helpers of the "Bird's Nest," while they don't show a loving spirit, a kind spirit, in their own homes towards their fathers, mothers, sisters, and brothers. My dear children, every one of you should be a missionary at home. Try to be a Christian at home. Try to adorn Jesus Christ's doctrine at home. Strive to be like the Lord Jesus Christ. Keep His words in your minds. Walk in His steps in your own families towards your fathers

questions, and talked to them about their souls. When she came to the archbishop, she said, "Tell me, my good man, how many commandments are there?" "Oh," said he, "there are eleven, madam." And when he said "eleven," Mrs. Rutherford said, "Alas, what an ignorant man you are! Have you never been at school? Has no one ever taught you how many commandments there are?" Then she told him how Moses wrote the Ten Commandments, and how in the book of Exodus the Ten Commandments are all written down as plain as possible.

"How is it," said she, "that you are so ignorant?"

Usher held down his head, and said nothing for a time. But when she had done her questioning, he said very quietly, "There is a word in the gospel which says, 'A new commandment give I unto you, that ye love one another'; and I think that a commandment given by our Lord Jesus should be attended to as well as Moses'

Little Things

and mothers, and everyone else.

There is a commandment I often t
of, about which a great man once s
curious thing. There was in this cou
before you or I, or anyone now living,
a great man called Archbishop Ush
holy, godly, Christian archbishop.
archbishop resolved one day to pay a
to a very holy Scotch minister na
Samuel Rutherford. He wanted to see
in his private life, how he went on ir
family. So he went dressed as a com
laborer that they might not know who
was. He knocked at the door and a
very quietly for a night's lodging.

Mr. Rutherford was a good, kind n
and was in the habit of receiving stran
into his house. So the door was opened
Usher was allowed to have the nig
lodging. He was sent to the kitchen to
some supper. After supper was over, N
Rutherford, who made it a rule to quest
and teach the servants every eveni
asked any strangers who were pres

commandments, and one added to ten makes eleven." They soon discovered it was the great Archbishop Usher, and you may fancy how Mrs. Rutherford felt when she found it out!

Now, my dear children, I hope you will never forget the new commandment given by our Lord Jesus Christ. You are to show a loving spirit. You are to be willing to give up your own way, to be good-natured, to keep your tempers. This is love. This is practical religion. This is showing religion at home. This shows that when you go and ask for money to teach the commandments of God to poor children, you yourselves are trying to keep them.

Try, last of all, to honor all God's commandments in spirit as well as in letter. There is a place in London where they sell all sorts of things. It is called "Soho Bazaar." A lady one day took one of her children there, a little girl. The little girl was so pleased with what she saw that she was tempted to do what she ought not. She fell into temptation. I am afraid she did not really "pray" when she said her prayers in the morning. Well, when she got into the Bazaar, she saw some things which looked so very nice that she coveted them. So by and by as she passed one of the stalls, when her mother was engaged and she thought no one could see, she took up a toy and put it into her pocket. But oh, how heavy that pocket felt! Her conscience began to speak to her! How miserable she felt. Oh, that she had not taken that toy!

As they were coming back, her mother stopped to talk to the woman who kept the same stall, and the poor little girl pulled the toy out of her pocket and put it back without anybody seeing. She went home, and at night she said her prayers. She seemed unhappy. She was thinking of what she had done at the "Bazaar."

Her mother said, "My dear child, what is the matter? Do tell me." And as her mother spoke to her in a kind, loving way, her heart was melted, and she said, "Oh, mother, I have been so miserable today. I have not broken a commandment quite. But oh, mother, I have *cracked* a commandment," and then she told all. Oh, dear children, take care and don't crack any of the commandments.

The *new* commandment I have told you of is in the 13th chapter of John, the 34th verse: "Love one another." Remember that. If you wish to help this blessed "Bird's Nest," do not forget the new commandment, "Love one another." Every one of you can understand that. Proverbs 20:11 says, "Even a child may be known by his doings." We can soon tell when a little child is trying to keep Christ's new commandment.

Keep it whole—don't let it be cracked or scratched. May God help us all to keep it, with a new heart and a lively faith in Christ! Then when we stand at Christ's judgment seat, He will say, "Well done, good and faithful servants, enter ye into the joy of your Lord."

The Happy Little Girl

Dear children, would you like to know who was the happiest child I ever saw? Listen to me and I will tell you.

The happiest child I ever saw was a little girl whom I once met traveling in a railway carriage. We were both going on a journey to London, and we traveled a great many miles together. She was only eight years old, and she was quite blind. She had never been able to see at all. She had never seen the sun, the stars, the sky, the grass, the flowers, the trees, the birds, or any of those pleasant things which you see every day of your lives; but still she was quite happy.

She was by herself, poor little thing. She had no friends or relations to take care of her on the journey and be good to her; but she was quite happy and content. She said, when she got into the carriage, "Tell me how many people there are in the carriage;

I am quite blind and can see nothing."

A gentleman asked her if she was afraid.

"No," she said, "I am not frightened. I have traveled before and I trust in God; and people are always very good to me."

But I soon found out the reason why she was so happy. What do you think it was? She loved Jesus Christ and Jesus Christ loved her; she had sought Jesus Christ and she had found Him.

I began to talk to her about the Bible, and I soon saw she knew a great deal of it. She went to a school where the mistress used to read the Bible to her; and she was a good girl, and had remembered what her mistress had read.

Dear children, you cannot think how many things in the Bible this poor little blind girl knew. I only wish that every grown-up person in England knew as much as she did. But I must try and tell you some of them.

She talked to me about sin: how it first came into the world when Adam and Eve ate the forbidden fruit, and how it was to be seen everywhere now. "Oh," she said, "there are no really good people! The very best people in the world have many sins every day, and I am sure we all waste a good deal of time, if we do nothing else wrong. Oh, we are all such sinners! There is nobody who has not sinned a great many sins."

And then she talked about Jesus Christ. She told me about His agony in the garden of Gethsemane, about His sweating drops of blood, about the soldiers nailing Him to the cross, about the spear piercing His side, and blood and water coming out. "Oh," she said, "how very good it was of Him to die for us, and such a cruel death; how good He was to suffer so for our sins!"

And then she talked about wicked people. She told me she was afraid there were a great many in the world, and it made her very unhappy to see how many of her schoolmates and acquaintances went on. "But," she said, "I know the reason why they are so wicked; it is because they do not try to be good; they do not wish to be good; they do not ask Jesus to make them good."

I asked her what part of the Bible she liked best. She told me she liked all the history of Jesus Christ, but the chapters she was most fond of were the three last chapters of the book of Revelation. I had a Bible with me, and I took it out and read these chapters to her as we went along.

When I had finished, she began to talk about heaven. "Think," she said, "how nice it will be to be there. There will be no more sorrow, nor crying, nor tears. And then Jesus Christ will be there, for it says, 'The Lamb is the light thereof,' and we shall always be with Him. And beside this, there shall be no night there; they will need no candle nor light of the sun."

Dear children, just think of this poor little blind girl. Think of her taking pleasure in talking of Jesus Christ. Think of her rejoicing in the account of heaven, where there shall be no sorrow nor night.

I have never seen her since. She went to her own home in London, and I do not know whether she is alive or not; but I hope she is, and I have no doubt Jesus Christ has taken good care of her.

Dear children, are you as happy and as cheerful as she was? You are not blind—you have eyes, and can run about and see everything, and go where you like, and read as much as you please to yourselves. But are you as happy as this poor little blind girl?

Oh, if you wish to be happy in this world, remember my advice today—do as the little blind girl did: "Love Jesus Christ, and He will love you. Seek Him early and you shall find Him!"

No More Crying

"God shall wipe away all tears from their eyes; and there shall be no more death, neither sorrow nor crying, neither shall there be any more pain." Revelation 21:4

Beloved children, a Bible text stands at the top of this page. I would like you to read it over twice. I am going to tell you something which, I hope, will make you remember that text as long as you live.

I am going to tell you about three places of which the Bible says a great deal. It matters little what we know about some places. But it matters much to know something about the three places of which I am now going to speak.

First, there is a place where there is a great deal of crying. Second, there is a place where there is nothing else *but* crying. Third, there is a place where there is no crying at all.

Now, attend to me, and I will tell you a few things worth knowing.

1. First of all, there is a place where there is a great deal of crying.

What is that place? It is the world in which you and I live. It is a world full of beautiful and pleasant things—the sun shining by day and the stars by night; the blue hills looking up to heaven and the rolling sea ebbing and flowing; the broad, quiet lakes and the rushing, restless rivers; the flowers blooming in the spring and the fields full of corn in autumn; the birds singing in the woods, and the lambs playing in the meadows—all these are beautiful things. I could look at them for hours and say, "What a beautiful world it is!" But still it is a world where there is a great deal of crying. It is a world where there are many tears.

There was crying in Bible times. Hagar wept when she thought Ishmael was dying. Abraham mourned when Sarah died.

Joseph wept when his brothers sold him into Egypt. David wept when Absalom was killed. There was weeping at Jerusalem when good King Josiah was slain in battle. There was weeping at Bethlehem when Herod killed all the little children who were two years old. These things, and many like them, you will find in your Bibles.

There is crying now all over the world. Little babies cry when they want anything, or feel pain. Boys and girls cry when they are hurt, frightened, or corrected. Grown-up people cry sometimes when they are in trouble, or when they see those die whom they love. In short, wherever there is sorrow and pain, there is crying.

I dare say you have seen people come to church all dressed in black. That is called being "in mourning." Some relative or friend of these people is dead, and therefore they dress in black. Well, remember when you see people in mourning, somebody has been crying.

I dare say you have seen graves in churchyards, and have heard that when people die they are buried there. Some of them are very little graves not longer than you are. Well, remember that when those graves were made, and little coffins were let down into them, there was crying.

Children, did you ever think where all this crying came from? Did you ever consider how it first began? Did you ever hear how weeping and tears came into the world? God did not make crying—that is certain. All that God made was "very good." Listen to me and I will tell you how crying began.

Crying came into the world by reason of sin. Sin is the cause of all the weeping and tears and sorrow and pain which there are upon earth. All the crying began when Adam and Eve ate the forbidden fruit and became sinners. It was sin which brought into the world pain and sickness and death. It was sin which brought into the world selfishness and ill nature and unkindness and quarreling and stealing and fighting. If there had been no wickedness, there would have been no weeping. If there had been no sin, there would have been no crying."

See now, my beloved children, how much you ought to hate sin. All the unhappiness in the world came from sin. How strange and wonderful it is that any- one can take pleasure in sin! Do not let that be the case with you. Watch against sin. Fight with it. Avoid it. Do not listen to it. Take the advice of Saint Paul: "Abhor that which is evil." Take the advice of Solomon: "When sinners entice thee, consent thou not." Say to yourself every morning, "Sin caused crying, and so I will hate sin."

See again, my beloved children, how foolish it is to expect perfect happiness in this world! It is expecting what you will not find. The world is a place where there is much crying, and where things do not always go on pleasantly. I hear many boys and girls talking of the pleasures they will have when they are men and women. I am sorry for them when I hear them talking in this way. I know they are mistaken. I know they will be disappointed. They will find when they grow up that they cannot get through the world without many troubles and cares. There are no roses without thorns. There are no years without dark and rainy days. There is no living on earth without crying and tears.

2. I will now speak of the second place about which I promised to tell you something. There is a place where there is nothing else but crying"

What is this place? It is the place where all bad people go when they are dead. It is the place which the Bible calls hell. In hell there is no laughter and smiling. There is nothing but "weeping and wailing and gnashing of teeth." In hell there is no happiness. Those who go there cry night and day without stopping. They have no rest. They never go to sleep and wake up happy. They never stop crying in hell.

Beloved children, I am sorry to tell you that there are many people going to hell. "Broad is the way that leadeth unto destruction," and many there are who go in it. I am afraid that many children are going to hell. I see many boys and girls who are so naughty and ill-behaved that I am sure they are not fit for heaven. And if they are not fit for heaven, where will they go if they die? There is only one other place to which they can go. They must go to hell.

Dear children, it makes me sad to say these things. I cannot bear the thought of boys and girls going to that dreadful place where there is nothing but crying. My heart's desire and prayer to God for you is that you may not go to hell. But I want you to know some things which you must mind if you would not go to hell. Listen to me now while I ask you a few questions.

For one thing, I will ask you, "Do you love Jesus Christ?" You ought to love Him. He died for your sins upon the cross that He might save you from hell. He allowed

Himself to be shut up in the dark prison of the grave that your sins might be forgiven, and that you might not be chained in hell forever. Dear children, think about this! If you love nothing but play and eating and drinking and fine clothes and storybooks, and do not love Christ, you are not in the right way. Take care. If you do not mind, you will go at last to the place where there is nothing but crying.

I will ask you another thing: "Do you try to please Christ?" You ought to do so. I read in the Bible that Jesus Christ said, "If ye love Me, keep My commandments," and, "Ye are my friends, if ye do whatsoever I command you." Dear children, think about this! If you are selfish or passionate or tell lies or quarrel with one another or do not do as you are bid, you are not Christ's friends. Take care. If you do not mind, you will go at last to the place where there is nothing but crying"

I will ask you another thing: "Do you keep Sunday holy?" You ought to do so.

God commands it, and it is for your good. I once heard of a little boy who went to play upon the ice on Sunday instead of coming home straight from church. "Tommy," said his mother, "why did you do so?"

"Mother," said Tommy, "I did not remember that it was Sunday."

"Tommy," said his mother, "that is the very thing God told you to do. He said in the fourth commandment, 'Remember to keep holy the Sabbath.' "

Dear children, think about this! If you do not like to give God one day in the week, your hearts are not right. Take care. If you do not mind, you will go at last to the place where there is nothing but crying"

I will ask you another thing: "Do you say your prayers?" You ought to do so. God will never be a friend to you if you do not speak to Him and ask Him to take care of your soul and make you good. If you never pray, or say your prayers without thinking, your heart will soon be full of mischief and sin. It will never be empty for a day. I once heard of a boy who had a little garden given to him all full of flowers. But he did nothing for it. He never raked it or weeded it. After a few weeks the weeds came up so thick that the flowers died. Dear children, think of this! If you do not ask God to put the Holy Spirit in your hearts, the devil will soon fill them with sin. Take care. If you do not mind, you will go at last to the place where there is nothing but crying.

I will ask you one more question: "Do you read your Bible?" You ought to do so. That beautiful book is able to keep you from hell and save your soul. If you use the Bible rightly, you will not be hurt by the devil.

I once heard of a little boy in Africa who was sleeping with his father in the open air near a fire. He awoke in the middle of the night and saw a great lion close to him, looking as if he was going to seize him. The little boy took up a lighted stick out of the fire and put it in the lion's face, and drove him away. Dear children, think of this!

The devil is a roaring lion, seeking whom he may devour. But he cannot harm you if you make a right use of the Bible. If you would drive him from you, you must read your Bible. If you can read and yet neglect your Bible, you are in great danger. Take care. If you do not mind, the devil will carry you off to the place where there is nothing but crying.

Beloved children, remember my five questions. Think of them often, and try your own hearts by them. I am not afraid for children who love Jesus and try to please Him, and keep Sunday holy, and pray and read their Bibles. I am not afraid that they will go to hell if they die. But I am afraid about children who care nothing about these things. I think they are in great danger.

3. I will now speak of the third place about which I promised to tell you something. There is a place where there is no crying at all.

What is this place? It is heaven. It is the place to which all good people go when they are dead. There all is joy and happiness. There no tears are shed. There sorrow and pain and sickness and death can never enter in. There can be no crying in heaven because there is nothing that can cause grief.

Dear children, there will be no more lessons in heaven. All will have been learned. The school will be closed. The rod and correction will be laid aside forever. There will be an eternal holiday.

There will be no more work in heaven. Man will no longer need to labor for his bread. The head will no longer have to ache with thinking. The hands will no longer be stiff and brown with toiling. There will be an eternal rest for the people of God.

There will be no sickness in heaven. Pain and disease and weakness and death will not be known. The people who dwell there shall no more say, "I am sick." They

will be always well. There will be nothing
but health and strength for evermore.

There will be no sin in heaven. There
will be no bad tempers, no unkind words,
no spiteful actions. The great tempter, the
devil, will not be allowed to come in and
spoil the happiness. There shall be nothing
but holiness and love for evermore.

Best of all, the Lord Jesus Christ Himself
will be in the midst of heaven. His people
shall at last see Him face to face, and go
out from His presence no more. He shall
gather His lambs into His bosom, and wipe
away all tears from all eyes. Where He is
will be fullness of joy, and at His right hand
shall be pleasures for evermore.

Dear children, would you not like to go
to heaven? We cannot live always in this
world. A day will come when we must die,
like the old people who have died already.
Children, would you like to go to heaven
when you die? Listen to me, and I will tell
you something about the way by which you
must go.

If you would go to heaven, you must have your sins forgiven and your hearts made new and good. There is only One who can do this for you. That One is the Lord Jesus Christ. God has appointed Him to be the Friend of sinners. He can wash away your sins in His own precious blood. He can make your hearts new by putting the Holy Spirit in them. He is the Way and the Door into heaven. He has the keys in His hand. Children, if you want to go to heaven, you must ask Jesus Christ to let you in.

Ask Jesus in prayer to get ready a place for you in that world where there is no crying. Ask Him to put your name in His book of life and to make you one of His people. Ask Him to cleanse you from all your sins and to put the Holy Ghost in your heart. Ask Him to give you power to fight the battle against sin, the world, and the devil. Ask Him to give you grace to make you good while you are young, and then good when you grow up, so that you may be safe while you live and happy forever when you die.

Children, Jesus Christ is ready to do all this if you will only ask Him. He has done it for many people already. He is waiting to do it for you at this very time. Do not be afraid to ask Him. Tell Him you have heard that He was very kind to people when He was on earth, and ask Him to be kind to you. Remind Him how kind He was to the poor, dying thief on the cross. Say to Him, "Lord Jesus, remember me; I want to go to heaven. Lord, think upon me. Lord, give me the Holy Spirit. Lord, pardon my sins and give me a new heart. Lord Jesus, save me."

And now, children, I have kept my word. I have told you of three places:

I have told you of a place where there is nothing but crying. I hope none of you will go there.

I have told you of a place where there is no crying. I hope you will all go there.

I have told you of a place where there is

a great deal of crying. That place is the world in which you are living.

Would you like, last of all, to know the best way to be happy in this world? Listen to me and I will tell you.

The happiest people in this world are those who make the Bible the rule of their lives. They read their Bibles often. They believe what the Bible says. They love that Savior, Jesus Christ, of whom the Bible speaks. They try to obey what the Bible commands. None are so happy as these people. They cannot prevent sickness and trouble from coming to them at times. But they learn from the Bible to bear them patiently. Children, if you would get through the world happily, make the Bible your best friend.

Shall I tell you a story that I once heard about a little boy and the Bible? Perhaps it will help you to remember what I have just been saying. I want the words I have just written to stick forever in your minds.

"Father," said this little boy one day, "I

do not see any use in reading the Bible. I do not see that it does people any good."

Little Johnny said this in a rather cross and peevish way, and his father thought it best not to begin reasoning with him. "Johnny," he said, "put on your hat, and come out and take a walk with me."

Johnny's father took him first to a house where there was an old woman who was very poor, and he talked to her about her poverty. "Sir," said the old woman, "I do not complain. I have read in the Bible these words, 'I have learned in whatsoever state I am therewith to be content.'"

"Johnny," said the little boy's father, "hear what the old woman says."

They went on to another house where there was a young woman who was very ill, and never likely to get better. Johnny's father asked her if she felt afraid to die. "No!" she said, "I find it written in the Bible, 'Though I walk through the valley of the shadow of death, I will fear no evil, for Thou art with me.'"

"Johnny," said the little boy's father again, "hear what the young woman says."

Children, when Johnny and his father came home that afternoon from their walk, his father asked him one question: "Johnny, do you think it is of any use to read the Bible? Do you think reading the Bible does people any good?"

And now what do you think Johnny said? I will tell you. He held down his head, and said nothing. But his face got very red, and he looked very much ashamed.

Children, from that very day Johnny was never heard again to say, "It is of no use reading the Bible."

Beloved children, remember my parting words. The way to get through the world with the least possible crying is to read the Bible, believe the Bible, pray over the Bible, and live by the Bible.

He who goes through life in this way will have the least crying in this world. And best of all, he will have no crying at all in the world to come.

Other Books for the Family
Published by Soli Deo Gloria

James W. Alexander
Thoughts on Family Worship

John Angell James
Female Piety
Addresses to Young Men
A Help to Domestic Happiness
The Widow Directed to the Widow's God
The Christian Father's Present to His Children

James Janeway/Cotton Mather
A Token for Children bound with
A Token for the Children of New England

J. G. Pike
Persuasives to Early Piety
A Guide for Young Disciples

Charles Haddon Spurgeon
A Good Start

For a complete listing of titles, write or call:

Soli Deo Gloria
P.O. Box 451
Morgan, PA 15064
(412) 221-1901/FAX 221-1902